olive

101 EASY ENTERTAINING IDEAS

1 3 5 7 9 10 8 6 4 2

Published in 2008 by BBC Books, an imprint of Ebury Publishing
A Random House Group company

The Random House Group Limited Reg. No. 954009

Addresses for companies within the Random House Group can be found at
www.randomhouse.co.uk

A CIP catalogue record for this book is available from the British Library.

The Random House Group Limited supports The Forest Stewardship Council
(FSC), the leading international forest certification organization.
All our titles that are printed on Greenpeace approved FSC certified paper
carry the FSC logo. Our paper procurement policy can be found at
www.rbooks.co.uk/environment

To buy books by your favourite authors and register for offers visit
www.rbooks.co.uk

Printed and bound by Firmengruppe APPL, aprinta druck, Wemding, Germany
Colour origination by Dot Gradations Ltd, UK

Commissioning Editor: Lorna Russell
Project Editor: Laura Higginson
Designer: Kathryn Gammon
Production: Lucy Harrison
Picture Researcher: Gabby Harrington

ISBN: 978 1846 07570 4

olive

101 EASY ENTERTAINING IDEAS

Editor
Janine Ratcliffe

BOOKS

Contents

Introduction

At **olive** we think entertaining should be a breeze. It should be about sharing gorgeous food with friends, not slaving for hours in the kitchen over complicated recipes. So whether you are having a casual lunch, an after-work supper for friends or a full-on dinner party you will find all the recipes you need here for a fuss-free menu.

With an emphasis on simple, stylish dishes with a wow factor these imaginative recipes are guaranteed to impress, without making huge demands on your time and effort.

In *101 Easy Entertaining Ideas* there are recipes to cover every occasion so if you want a make-ahead starter, a one-pot main or a throw together pudding then this is where you'll find them. For this collection the **olive** team has picked out simple but stunning dishes like *Roast duck legs with sweet potato mash* (pictured opposite, see page 70 for the recipe), which will impress even the most discerning guest.

As always, all the recipes have been thoroughly tested in the **olive** kitchen to make sure they taste fabulous and work for you first time.

Janine Ratcliffe

Janine Ratcliffe
Food Editor
olive magazine

Notes and Conversions

NOTES ON THE RECIPES

• Where possible, we use humanely reared meats, free-range chickens and eggs, and unrefined sugar.

• Eggs are large unless stated otherwise. Pregnant women, elderly people, babies and toddlers, and anyone who is unwell should avoid eating raw and partially cooked eggs.

APPROXIMATE WEIGHT CONVERSIONS

• All the recipes in this book are listed with metric measurements.

• Cup measurements, which are used by cooks in Australia and America, have not been listed here as they vary from ingredient to ingredient. Please use kitchen scales to measure dry/solid ingredients.

OVEN TEMPERATURES

gas	°C	fan °C	°F	description
¼	110	90	225	Very cool
½	120	100	250	Very cool
1	140	120	275	Cool or slow
2	150	130	300	Cool or slow
3	160	140	325	Warm
4	180	160	350	Moderate
5	190	170	375	Moderately hot
6	200	180	400	Fairly hot
7	220	200	425	Hot
8	230	210	450	Very hot
9	240	220	475	Very hot

SPOON MEASURES

Spoon measurements are level unless otherwise specified.

• 1 teaspoon (tsp) = 5ml

• 1 tablespoon (tsp) = 15ml

• 1 Australian tablespoon = 20ml (cooks in Australia should measure 3 teaspoons where 1 tablespoon is specified in a recipe)

APPROXIMATE LIQUID CONVERSIONS

metric	imperial	US
60ml	2fl oz	¼ cup
125ml	4fl oz	½ cup
175ml	6fl oz	¾ cup
225ml	8fl oz	1 cup
300ml	10fl oz/½ pint	1¼ cups
450ml	16fl oz	2 cups/1 pint
600ml	20fl oz/1 pint	2½ cups
1 litre	35fl oz/1¾ pints	1 quart

Please note that an Australian cup is 250ml, ¾ cup is 190ml, ½ cup is 125ml, ¼ cup is 60ml.

Goat's cheese and red onion tarts

50 minutes

shortcrust pastry 500g block
red onions 2 large
olive oil for frying and drizzling
balsamic vinegar 1 tbsp
thyme leaves chopped, ½ tbsp
goat's cheese 6 slices, from a small log

■ Heat the oven to 200C/fan 180C/ gas 6. Line 6 tart tins (about 10cm across) with pastry and prick the bases. Line with parchment and baking beans, and bake for 10 minutes or until the pastry starts to brown, lift out the parchment and bake for another 5 minutes or until the pastry is crisp, dried and cooked.

■ Meanwhile, slice the red onions thickly (you need 6 fat slices). Heat a little oil in a large frying pan and carefully fry the slices, without breaking them, on each side until they start to soften, about 15 minutes in total. Add the balsamic vinegar and thyme, and bubble together. Lift a slice of onion into each tart and put a slice of goat's cheese on top.

■ Bake until the goat's cheese begins to bubble and brown a little. Drizzle with a little olive oil before serving. **Makes 6**

This recipe uses large red onions so that a slice fills each pastry case. If you can only find small ones, just overlap two slices.

Prawn cocktail
10 minutes

large cooked peeled prawns 300g
Little Gem lettuce 2 heads, leaves separated
cayenne or **paprika** a large pinch
large cooked prawns in shells, to garnish
    (optional)
lime or **lemon wedges** to serve

MARIE ROSE SAUCE
mayonnaise 4 tbsp
tomato ketchup 1½ tbsp
Tabasco sauce a dash
fresh lemon juice 1 tbsp

■ Mix together all the sauce ingredients, adding more Tabasco or lemon if you like.
■ Arrange the Little Gem leaves in pretty glasses. Pile on the prawns, spoon over some sauce and sprinkle each with a tiny pinch of cayenne. Garnish with prawns in shells (if using) and serve with lime or lemon wedges. **Serves 4**

Tomato ketchup, although not a usual cooking ingredient, is vital in this recipe – Marie Rose sauce never tastes right with anything else.

Veggie tempura

25 minutes

soda water 250ml, ice cold
tempura flour 150g (or use plain flour)
groundnut oil for deep frying
shiitake mushrooms 150g, sliced
sweet potato 1, halved lengthways and
  thinly sliced
aubergine 1, thinly sliced
red pepper 1, cut into strips

PONZU DIPPING SAUCE
fresh lemon juice 4 tbsp
soy sauce 4 tbsp
caster sugar 1 tbsp

■ Mix together the ponzu sauce ingredients. Pour the soda water into a bowl, add the flour and lightly mix until batter just combined (you want it a bit lumpy).

■ Fill a wok or pan ⅓ full with oil and heat. Test the heat by dropping in a piece of bread – if it sizzles and floats to the top, the oil is hot enough. Dip the vegetables in the batter and drop into the oil in batches. Fry until golden, then drain on kitchen paper. Serve with the sauce. **Serves 6**

You can use any combination of vegetables for this – the trick is to slice them very thinly. Buy tempura flour from Japanese supermarkets.

Poached egg on green beans with ravigote sauce

15 minutes

green beans 200g, trimmed
extra-virgin olive oil 3 tbsp
red wine vinegar 1 tsp
Dijon mustard 2 tsp
capers 1 tsp, chopped
flat-leaf parsley leaves chopped, 2 tbsp
tarragon leaves a handful, chopped
shallot 1, finely chopped
white wine vinegar 1 tbsp
eggs 4

■ Blanch the beans in salted water until al dente. Drop into iced water, drain and toss in 1 tsp of the oil. Whisk the red wine vinegar with the mustard, season, and pour in the rest of the oil while whisking. Stir in the capers, herbs and shallot.

■ Just before serving, reheat the beans. Bring 5cm of water to a simmer in a shallow pan with the white wine vinegar.

■ Crack each egg into a cup and gently slide into the pan. Cook for 3–4 minutes until set. Remove with a slotted spoon and drain on kitchen paper. Divide the beans among 4 plates, top with an egg and pour dressing over each. **Serves 4**

To keep your egg whites firm and without ragged edges, use really fresh eggs and add a little vinegar to the boiling water.

Prosciutto-wrapped scallops with lemon and parsley butter

40 minutes

cherry tomatoes on the vine 24

scallops 24 small, cleaned

prosciutto 12 slices, each cut into 2

extra-virgin olive oil 3 tbsp

butter 3 tbsp

garlic 2 cloves, finely chopped

lemon 1, zested and juiced

flat-leaf parsley a small bunch, finely
    chopped

■ Heat the oven to 180C/fan 160C/gas 4. Arrange the tomatoes on a baking sheet and season. Bake for 20 minutes, remove from oven and set aside. Reduce the heat to 120C/fan 100C/gas ½.

■ Put 1 scallop on each piece of prosciutto, roll up tightly and secure with a toothpick. Heat a frying pan until very hot.

■ Add the olive oil and sear the scallops until the prosciutto is browned and crisp on both sides. Keep warm in the oven while searing the rest.

■ Add the butter and garlic to the pan and cook for 2 minutes on a low heat. Add the lemon zest and juice and heat through. Add the parsley. Serve the scallops with the tomatoes and the garlic butter drizzled over. **Serves 8**

If your fishmonger sells scallops in shells, use the shell to serve. But first give them a good scrub, then sterilize in a hot oven for 10 minutes.

Cauliflower and Parmesan soup

30 minutes

---

onion 1 large, roughly chopped
garlic 2 cloves, roughly chopped
butter
cauliflower 1 head, roughly chopped
milk 750ml
Parmesan 50g, finely grated
fresh chives snipped into long lengths, to
    garnish
crusty bread to serve

■ Cook the onion and garlic in a large knob of butter until really soft. Add the cauliflower and cook for a minute then pour in the milk and simmer until the cauliflower is tender. Whiz in a blender until completely smooth. Stir in the Parmesan, season well and sprinkle with chives. Serve with crusty bread. **Serves 4**

When buying cauliflower look for firm, creamy-white, densely packed heads with crisp, green outer leaves.

Mussels with garlic and herb breadcrumbs

45 minutes

mussels 2kg, cleaned
butter 50g, frozen and grated
fresh breadcrumbs 50g
garlic 1 clove, crushed
parsley leaves a small bunch, chopped
lemon 1, cut into wedges, to serve
crusty bread warmed, to serve

■ Make sure all the mussels are alive before you cook them – if any are open, tap them on the work surface, if they don't close, throw them away.

■ Heat a large, wide pan, tip in the mussels with a splash of water, cover and cook until opened. Throw away any that won't open. Remove the top shell from each mussel and discard. Mix the butter, breadcrumbs, garlic and parsley together.

■ Put a layer of half mussel shells on a baking sheet. Sprinkle breadcrumb mix over each one then flash under a very hot grill until just golden. Serve with lemon and crusty bread. **Serves 2**

This is lovely eaten with crusty bread as a starter but you could also serve the mussels as canapés with drinks. Mussels are at their best in the colder months.

Scallops with pea and mint purée

20 minutes

frozen peas 250g
butter, 25g plus extra for frying
chicken stock 100ml
mint leaves 1 small bunch, roughly chopped
scallops 12
ground cumin ½ tsp
sunflower oil
salad leaves to garnish
balsamic vinegar to garnish

■ Put the peas, butter and stock in a pan and season well. Simmer for about 3–4 minutes (you want the peas to stay bright green) then tip into a food processor or blender with the mint and whiz to a purée. Put back in the pan and keep warm.

■ Season the scallops with a little cumin and salt. Heat a non-stick frying pan to very hot with a little oil and butter.

■ Sear the scallops for about 1 minute each side (you want a nice caramelized colour on them). Serve 3 scallops per person on a bed of the pea purée with a few leaves dressed with balsamic. **Serves 4**

This is a really quick but impressive-looking dish. The pea purée is quite soft, so it doubles up as a sauce.

Sweet potato and Cheshire cheese soufflés

1 hour 10 minutes

butter 25g, plus extra for buttering the ramekins

Parmesan 3 tbsp, finely grated

sweet potatoes 350g, peeled and cut into chunks

plain flour 2 tbsp

milk 150ml

Cheshire cheese 75g, crumbled

dried chilli flakes a pinch

fresh chives snipped, 1 tbsp

eggs 2, plus 2 egg whites

Try to get orange-fleshed sweet potatoes for this – they give a better colour to the finished dish.

■ Heat the oven to 200C/fan 180C/gas 6. Butter 6 x 200ml ramekins and dust the insides with Parmesan.

■ Cook the sweet potatoes in boiling salted water for 10–15 minutes, until tender. Drain and mash well.

■ Melt the butter in a pan and stir in the flour. Gradually add the milk, mixing well between each addition, until you have a smooth sauce. Add the cheese, stirring until melted, then stir in the chilli flakes and chives. Remove from the heat and fold in the mashed sweet potatoes. Cool.

■ Separate the eggs and stir the yolks into the sweet potato mixture. Put all the whites in a large bowl and whisk with an electric whisk until stiff. Fold a quarter of the egg whites into the sweet potato mixture to loosen it, then fold in the rest. Divide the mixture among the ramekins and put them on a baking sheet. Bake for 20–25 minutes, until risen and golden.

Serves 6

Hot-smoked salmon and watercress pâté with bagel crisps

15 minutes

hot-smoked salmon 250g, flaked
unsalted butter 100g, softened
soft cheese 100g
lemon 1, juiced
watercress a handful
wholemeal bagels 3
olive oil 2 tbsp
sea salt flakes

■ Put the salmon, butter, cream cheese, lemon juice and watercress in a food processor and whiz until roughly blended. Halve the bagels then slice thinly. Drizzle with olive oil and sea salt, and bake at 190C/fan 170C/gas 5 for 10–15 minutes or until crisp. Serve with the pâté. **Serves 6**

This pâté can be made a few hours or a day ahead and chilled until you need to use it.

Crystal herb rice paper rolls with peanut sauce

45 minutes

thin rice noodles 50g

rocket 50g

red onion 1 small, halved and sliced

carrots 2 large, cut into matchsticks

red pepper 1, cut into matchsticks

coriander leaves a handful, chopped

rice paper wrappers 12 (buy them from Asian grocers)

mint leaves 1 small bunch, stems discarded

PEANUT DIPPING SAUCE

hoisin sauce 5 tbsp

smooth peanut butter 3 tbsp

sesame oil 1 tbsp

chilli sauce or **chilli bean paste** 1 tsp

Buy rice paper noodle wrappers from Asian grocers. They are sold dried in packs and will need rehydrating before use – try to roll them as tight as possible without ripping for best results.

■ For the peanut sauce mix all ingredients together in a bowl. Add 3 tbsp boiling water, mix and pour into a serving bowl.

■ Pour boiling water over the noodles and leave for 3 minutes until soft. Rinse under cold water, drain and put on a clean tea towel and cut into pieces about 12 cm long with scissors.

■ Put the vegetables, herbs and noodles in separate piles on a tray.

■ Pour hot water into a bowl then drop in 1 rice paper and leave for about 30 seconds until softened. Remove and drain off the excess water with kitchen paper. Put 2 mint leaves on the top portion of the wrapper and a small amount of each of the vegetables, coriander and noodles across the lower middle of the circle. Bring up the lower part of the rice circle over the vegetables and then fold in the sides. Roll up into a tight spring roll. Put seam-side down on a tray then repeat for the other wrappers.

■ Serve the rolls whole or cut diagonally just before serving with a very sharp knife. Serve with the peanut dipping sauce.

Makes 12 rolls

Manchego and fresh fig chutney for crostini

30 minutes

red onion 1, finely chopped

soft brown sugar 4 tbsp

mustard seeds 1 tsp

cinnamon stick

star anise 1

ginger root thumb-sized piece, grated

red wine vinegar 4 tbsp

figs 4, cut into wedges

French stick 12 thin slices, drizzled with
    olive oil and toasted

Manchego cheese 100g, shaved

rocket a handful, to garnish

■ Put the onion, sugar, spices, ginger and vinegar in a pan and cook together slowly until the onion is completely softened. Add the fig wedges and cook for another 5–10 minutes until the figs are just starting to break down. To serve, top the crostini with a little Manchego, some fig chutney and a couple of rocket sprigs. **Serves 4**

Once ripe, figs will deteriorate very quickly, so eat them straightaway if possible.

Salt and pepper squid

25 minutes

Szechuan peppercorns 1 tbsp
dried chilli flakes 1 tsp
sea salt flakes 1 tbsp
plain flour 4 tbsp
cornflour 4 tbsp
squid 400g, cleaned
groundnut oil for deep frying
lemon wedges to serve

■ Crush together the peppercorns, chilli flakes and sea salt with a pestle and mortar then mix with the flours. Slit the squid hoods down 1 side, open out then score the inside lightly in a criss-cross pattern. Cut into bite-sized pieces. Fill a large pan or wok 1/3 full with oil. Heat until a cube of bread browns in 30 seconds. Coat the squid pieces in the flour mix, shaking off the excess, and fry for 1–2 minutes or until golden.
■ Serve with lemon wedges. **Serves 2**

Squid has a fairly short season from the end of August to November. Buy from good fishmongers and larger supermarkets, and ask them to clean it for you.

Asparagus, mozzarella and prosciutto parcels

20 minutes

asparagus 16 spears, trimmed
mozzarella 125g ball, sliced into 4
prosciutto 8–12 slices
olive oil 3 tbsp, plus extra for frying
red wine vinegar 1 tbsp
basil leaves 1 small bunch, finely shredded
salad leaves to serve

■ Blanch the asparagus for 2 minutes then refresh under cold water. Cut each mozzarella slice in half and sit both pieces on top of 2 spears of asparagus. Top with 2 more spears then wrap the asparagus in prosciutto so the mozzarella is enclosed (you will need 2 or 3 strips). Heat a little olive oil in a pan, then carefully fry the parcels until the prosciutto has crisped and the mozzarella oozes.

■ Whisk together the olive oil and vinegar and add the basil.

■ Serve each parcel with salad leaves and a little dressing drizzled over. **Serves 4**

Asparagus will snap at the point where it becomes woody. Use the trimmings in a vegetable stock to avoid waste.

Smoked mackerel, lemon and herb pâté

15 minutes

smoked mackerel 250g, skin and bones
removed, flaked
soft cheese 200g
lemon 1, zested and juiced
fresh parsley and **chives** chopped and
snipped, 2 tbsp each
horseradish cream or **sauce** 1–2 tbsp, to
taste
melba toast or **toasted brioche**
to serve

■ Put the smoked mackerel, cheese,
lemon zest and juice in a food processor
and whiz until blended. Stir in the herbs
and horseradish. Chill until ready to serve.
Serves 6

To make melba toast, toast thick slices of
white bread, cut off the crusts and slice
horizontally to get 2 thin pieces. Grill the
untoasted sides until golden and crisp.

Grilled goat's cheese with walnut and parsley pesto

15 minutes

shelled walnuts 25g, toasted
flat-leaf parsley 1 small bunch
garlic 1 clove, crushed
olive oil
lemon ½, juiced
goat's cheese 4 thick slices, from a log (with a rind)
salad leaves to serve

■ Put the walnuts, parsley and garlic in a food processor. Whiz together, adding olive oil, until you have a spoonable consistency. Season and add the lemon juice.

■ Put the goat's cheese on a non-stick baking sheet and slide under the grill until golden.

■ Serve the goat's cheese on the salad leaves and spoon over the pesto. **Serves 4**

All nuts will get drier and more bitter with age. Look for new-season walnuts in the autumn – they will give you a sweeter pesto.

Pork, apricot and pistachio terrine

**1½ hours + marinating + chilling over
2 nights**

pork tenderloin fillet 300g, trimmed of fat
and diced
garlic 2 cloves, crushed
fresh thyme 2 sprigs
brandy 2 tbsp
dry-cured rashers rindless streaky bacon
250g
sausagemeat 1kg, buy good quality or use
skinned sausages
parsley leaves 1 small bunch, chopped
fresh chives 1 small bunch, snipped
shelled pistachios 100g pack
dried apricots 8–10

**You can press the terrine as it cools in the
fridge using a board with a couple of tins
on top. This will give a firmer texture.**

■ Put the pork, garlic, 1 thyme sprig and
the brandy in a bowl, cover and leave to
marinate overnight in the fridge.

■ Heat the oven to 180C/fan 160C/gas 4.
Butter a 1kg terrine mould or loaf tin, put
the remaining sprig of thyme in the bottom
and line it with overlapping strips of bacon,
leaving any extra hanging over the edge.
Loosen the sausagemeat with a fork, add it
to the bowl with the marinated pork and
mix well. Stir through the parsley, chives
and pistachios, and season well. Pack the
terrine with half of the pork mixture and
lay the apricots in a row down the centre.
Pack the remaining pork on top, flatten and
stretch over the bacon. Cover with buttered
foil and wrap the whole terrine in a double
layer of cling film.

■ Put the terrine in a roasting tin half filled
with boiling water and bake for 1 hour. Cool
and chill overnight. Release the terrine by
dipping it briefly in hot water and turning
it out on to a plate. **Serves 8**

Fig, gorgonzola and prosciutto salad

10 minutes

olive oil 3 tbsp
balsamic vinegar 1 tbsp
ripe figs 4, halved
Gorgonzola or **dolcelatte** 100g, sliced
prosciutto 6 slices
watercress 1 bunch, stems removed

■ Whisk together the olive oil with the balsamic vinegar and season with pepper. Arrange the figs, cheese, prosciutto and watercress on 2 plates. Drizzle with the dressing and serve. **Serves 2**

The cheese and prosciutto are both very salty so just use pepper to season this.

Sugar-cured salmon
30 minutes + 24-hour curing

salmon fillet 1, about 500–800g, skin on
and bones removed
rock salt 100g
light muscovado sugar 100g
star anise 2, roughly crushed
orange 1, zested, save the juice for the
dressing
vodka 3 tbsp

HERB SALAD AND DRESSING
lamb's lettuce 50g bag
rocket 50g bag
chervil leaves 1 bunch, roughly chopped
fresh chives bunch, snipped
olive oil 3 tbsp
Dijon mustard 1 tsp
cider vinegar 1 tbsp
light muscovado sugar ½ tsp

■ Lay the salmon on a non-metal tray or plate skin-side down. Mix together the salt, sugar, star anise and orange zest, and spread the mixture over the salmon flesh. Sprinkle over the vodka. Wrap the lot in cling film, then put a board on top and weigh it down with a couple of tins. Leave for 24 hours, but every few hours tip off any liquid that collects.

■ When ready, unwrap and brush off the sugar and salt mix (give it a quick rinse if needed). Slice the salmon thinly on the diagonal. Arrange on plates. Toss the salad leaves and herbs together, whisk the olive oil with the orange juice, mustard, vinegar and sugar and dress the leaves.

■ Serve with the salmon. **Serves 12**

Use a plastic tray or ceramic plate when curing the salmon, as the cure could react with metal.

Roasted carrot soup with herb crème fraîche

1 hour

---

onion 1, cut into wedges

carrots 800g, peeled and roughly chopped

butter

bay leaf 1

clear honey 1 tsp

vegetable or **chicken stock** 2 litres

crème fraîche 200ml

mint, basil and **chervil leaves** chopped, 4
tbsp (use any one or a mix of 2 or 3)

■ Heat the oven to 200C/fan 180C/gas 6 and put the onion and carrots in a roasting tin with a few knobs of butter. Roast for 30 minutes or until the veg are tinged brown. Tip into a pan, add the bay leaf, honey and stock and bring to a simmer.

■ Cook for 10 minutes or until the carrots are very tender, then remove the bay and whiz the lot in a blender until smooth.

■ Sieve if you'd like it really smooth. Season and keep warm.

■ Mix the crème fraîche and herbs and season. Serve the soup with quenelles of herbed crème fraîche. **Serves 6**

Roasting carrots concentrates their natural sugars and really brings out their sweet flavour.

Simple crab cakes with fennel remoulade

50 minutes

cooked white crab meat 400g
mayonnaise 3 tbsp
spring onion 2, finely chopped
flat-leaf parsley chopped, 3 tbsp
eggs 2, beaten
fresh breadcrumbs
butter for frying

FENNEL REMOULADE
fennel bulb 1, finely shredded
shallots 2 small, finely sliced
flat-leaf parsley chopped, 2 tbsp
mayonnaise 4 tbsp
Dijon mustard 2 tbsp
capers 1 tsp, rinsed
gherkins or **cornichons** chopped, 1 tbsp
lemon 1, juiced

■ Mix together the crab, mayo, spring onion and flat-leaf parsley. Form into 12 small cakes then dip in egg and coat in breadcrumbs. Put in the fridge for 30 minutes to firm up. Mix all the remoulade ingredients together.

■ Heat a knob of butter in a non-stick frying pan. Fry the crab cakes in batches until golden brown. Serve with the remoulade. **Serves 4**

Remoulade is a classic French sauce made with a piquantly flavoured mayo. It's often used to dress celeriac, but this is a lovely seasonal variation.

Mozzarella, prosciutto and Charentais melon salad

10 minutes

buffalo mozzarella 1 ball, torn into pieces
prosciutto 6 slices
Charentais melon 2 fat wedges, skin
    removed
olive oil
lemon a squeeze of juice

■ Arrange the mozzarella, prosciutto and melon on 2 plates.

■ Drizzle with olive oil and a squeeze of lemon juice. Sprinkle lightly with sea salt flakes and cracked black pepper. **Serves 2**

When buying the melon, apply gentle pressure to the stalk area – if it gives, it should be ready to eat. To prepare, cut in half then scoop out the seeds and fibrous bits.

Pea, feta and herb fritters

30 minutes

plain flour 100g
baking powder 1 tsp
egg 1
milk 150ml
frozen peas 100g, blanched for 2 minutes
    and drained
feta 100g, cut into small cubes
chives, parsley and **basil leaves** chopped, 2
    tbsp (use any one or a mix of 2 or 3)
spring onions 2, chopped
oil for frying
roasted cherry tomatoes on the vine to
    serve

■ Mix together the flour, baking powder, egg and milk to make a batter. Stir in the peas, feta, herbs and spring onions and season really well.

■ Heat a large non-stick frying pan with a little oil. Drop spoonfuls of the batter into the pan and cook for 2–3 minutes each side until golden and cooked through. Sprinkle with sea salt. Serve 3 per person with roasted cherry tomatoes on the side.

Serves 4

You can use fresh or frozen peas for this. If you use frozen just defrost thoroughly – there's no need to blanch them.

Crab, avocado and lime cocktails

20 minutes

cooked white crab meat 200g
coriander leaves chopped, 2 tbsp
red chilli 1, chopped
lime 1, juiced
rocket 2 handfuls
Hass avocados 2, peeled and sliced

LIME DRESSING
mayonnaise 150ml
lime 1, zested and juiced
coriander leaves chopped, 3 tbsp

■ Toss the crab with the coriander, chilli and lime juice. Season.
■ Divide the rocket leaves among 6 glasses. Layer the crab and avocado in each glass.
■ Mix the dressing ingredients, season and drizzle over the cocktails. **Serves 6**.

If you are buying crab to cook at home, choose one that feels heavy for its size. Alternatively, you can get the fishmonger to cook it for you, or many sell ready cooked crabs or crab meat.

Watercress soup with goat's cheese croûtes

40 minutes

onion 1, roughly chopped
garlic 1 clove, crushed
butter 25g
potato 1, peeled and cubed
vegetable or **chicken stock** 1 litre
watercress 250g, any really woody stalks
    removed
double cream 4 tbsp
small baguette 8 slices, toasted
goat's cheese 100g, sliced

■ Cook the onion and garlic in the butter until softened. Add the potato and stock and simmer for 15 minutes. Drop in the watercress and wilt for a minute or 2 (you want the soup to be bright green) then transfer to a blender and blend until smooth.

■ Pour back in the pan and stir in the cream. Season.

■ Top the baguette slices with goat's cheese and toast again. Pour the soup into bowls and top with a couple of goat's cheese croûtes. **Serves 4**

To store watercress, stand in a bowl of water, cover with a plastic bag.
Only remove the really fibrous woody stalks from the watercress. Everything else will blend to a smooth soup.

Crisp noodle-wrapped prawns with tomato jam

40 minutes

Chinese thin egg noodles 50g
large raw prawns with tails, 16, peeled
egg white 1
vegetable oil for frying

TOMATO JAM
tomatoes 5 large, quartered
red chillies 2, roughly chopped
garlic 3 cloves
root ginger 4cm, peeled and roughly
    chopped
fish sauce 2 tbsp
soft brown sugar 75g
red wine vinegar 3 tbsp

■ Purée the tomato-jam ingredients in a food processor until smooth. Pour into a small pan, add 4 tbsp water and simmer until thick (about 30 minutes).

■ Boil the noodles in salted water for 2 minutes. Rinse in cold water and then drain and leave to dry on a tea towel.

■ Brush each prawn with egg white and then wrap a couple of noodles around each prawn until it is covered to the tail.

■ Season and put on a tray. Heat about 5cm oil in a wok or small pan until hot but not smoking (a cube of bread will brown in 30 seconds). Fry the prawns for 1 minute or until golden and then drain on kitchen paper. Serve with the tomato jam as a dipping sauce. **Serves 4**

It's best to undercook the noodles so they don't break while wrapping. Serve with a spicy leaf such as mizuna or rocket.

Purple sprouting broccoli with prosciutto and duck egg

30 minutes

prosciutto 8 slices
purple sprouting broccoli 500g
olive oil for drizzling
balsamic vinegar for drizzling
Parmesan or **Grana Padano** a handful of, grated
duck's (or hen's) eggs 4, poached

■ Grill the prosciutto until crisp. Steam the broccoli until just tender, but still bright green – test a stalk with the point of a knife. Divide among 4 shallow bowls and drizzle with a little olive oil and balsamic.

■ Top the broccoli with pieces of crisp prosciutto and Parmesan. Poach the duck eggs in a frying pan of simmering water for 3–4 minutes or until cooked to your liking (2–3 minutes for hen's eggs). Lift out, drain and add an egg to each bowl.

■ Sprinkle with sea salt flakes and black pepper and serve. **Serves 4**

Early season purple sprouting broccoli can be cooked whole but any late grown may need to have the stalk peeled.

Crisp pork belly with spiced apricots

1 hour 15 minutes

boneless pork belly 1kg piece, skin scored
Chinese five-spice, 1 tbsp
brown sugar 2 tsp
dried apricots 12, halved
dried chilli flakes 1
cinnamon stick 1
greens 500g spring greens, chard or kale,
    steamed, to serve

■ Heat the oven to 200C/fan 180C/gas 6. If your piece of pork is not already scored, score diagonal lines across it with a very sharp knife (a Stanley knife works well). Mix the five-spice with the sugar and rub it well into the pork skin. Put the belly skin-side up in a shallow roasting tin and roast for about 1 hour or until it's cooked through and the crackling's crisp (if it isn't, briefly flash the pork under a hot grill). Rest for 15 minutes before serving.

■ While the pork is cooking, put the apricots, chilli (left whole) and cinnamon in a pan with 100ml water and bring to a simmer, then cook with the lid on for 8 minutes or until the apricots are very soft. Take the lid off and cook until any liquid has almost evaporated. Cut the pork into 4 squares and serve with greens and the spiced apricots. **Serves 4**

Pork belly is a good, cheap cut that cooks well and produces fantastic crackling. To help it crackle, make sure the skin is really dry.

Baked Brie in puff pastry

1 hour

baby Brie or **Coulommiers** 300g
puff pastry 500g block (use an all-butter puff for a better flavour)
tomato or **shallot chutney** 1 tbsp
egg 1 yolk, beaten
salad leaves dressed in vinaigrette, to serve

This can be prepared ahead, chilled in the fridge and baked at the last minute; you will need to give an extra 5–10 minutes in the oven.

■ Heat the oven to 220C/fan 200C/gas 7. Take the cheese out of the fridge and unwrap it before you start. Cut the pastry in half and roll out each piece on a floured surface – make 1 about 1 cm bigger than the cheese all the way around and the other slightly thinner and about 3cm bigger than the cheese all the way around.

■ Put the smaller pastry sheet on to a baking sheet and put the cheese in the middle. Spread the chutney on top of the cheese. Dampen the pastry around the cheese with water. Lay the other sheet on top, smooth down and press the top pastry sheet on to the bottom one. Trim around the edge with a sharp knife, leaving a 1 cm-border and rough the sides of the pastry up. Brush with the egg yolk and score lines in a swirling pattern from the centre of the pastry outwards.

■ Bake for 10 minutes and then turn down the oven to 180C/fan 160C/gas 4 and cook for 20 minutes or until the pastry is golden and puffed. Leave it to rest for 10 minutes before cutting it. Cut into quarters and serve with the salad leaves. **Serves 4**

Five-spice, ginger and soy poussins

1 hour 10 minutes

---

poussins 3
honey 4 tbsp
Chinese five-spice 1 tsp
vegetable oil
garlic 5 cloves, peeled and sliced
root ginger 1 thumb-sized piece, cut into
    matchsticks
chicken stock 250ml
red wine 125ml
soy sauce 100ml
spring onions 4, sliced, to garnish
red chillies 2, finely sliced, to garnish

■ Heat the oven to 180C/fan 160C/gas 4. Season the poussins, put in a large roasting dish and drizzle with the honey and five-spice. Heat 2 tbsp oil in a pan, fry the garlic and ginger for 2 minutes, then add all the liquids. Simmer for 10 minutes then pour over the poussins and cover with foil.

■ Roast for 30 minutes, then remove the foil, turn the oven up to 220C/fan 200C/gas 7 and cook for another 20 minutes.

■ Cut each poussin in half with a sharp knife or kitchen scissors and spoon over some of the sauce. Sprinkle with the spring onions and chillies. **Serves 6**

Poussins are just very young chickens – look out for free-range ones when buying.

Roast duck legs with sweet potato mash

1½ hours

---

duck legs 6, pricked all over with a fork
shallots 12
bay leaves 2
allspice ¼ tsp
white wine 300ml
parsley 1 small bunch, chopped, to garnish

SWEET POTATO MASH
sweet potatoes 1kg, peeled and cut
   into chunks
butter
whole nutmeg

■ Heat the oven to 190C/fan 170C/gas 5. Put the duck legs in a single layer in a large roasting tin and tuck the shallots and bay leaves around the legs. Mix the allspice with ½ tsp salt and sprinkle a little on each leg. Roast for 1 hour.

■ Spoon off almost all the fat (save it for roast potatoes if you like), then add the wine and return to the oven for 20 minutes to finish cooking.

■ Meanwhile, steam or simmer the sweet potato until tender, then mash with a large knob of butter and a grating of nutmeg and season well. Put a scoop of mash on each plate and lean a duck leg up against it, spoon some shallots and sauce around it and sprinkle with parsley. **Serves 6**.

Duck legs are a much cheaper option than duck breasts and are really easy to cook.

Thai-style mussels

30 minutes

mussels 2 kg, cleaned
spring onions 6, roughly chopped
lemon grass 2 stems, woody outer layers
    removed and roughly chopped
ginger root 1 thumb-sized piece, roughly
    chopped
garlic 2 cloves, peeled
green chillies 4, roughly chopped
fresh coriander 1 large bunch with roots
groundnut oil
coconut milk 400ml can
fish sauce 2 tbsp
lime 1, juiced
red chilli 1, finely sliced, to garnish

■ Tap any open mussels and discard those that don't close.

■ Put the spring onions, lemon grass, ginger, garlic, green chillies and coriander roots in a food processor and whiz to a paste. Add a splash of water if it's needed.

■ Heat 2 tbsp groundnut oil in a large, wide pan with a lid. Fry the paste for 2–3 minutes. Add the coconut milk, fish sauce and lime juice, and bring to a simmer. Add the mussels, put on the lid and steam for 3–4 minutes until all the mussels are open. Discard any that stay closed. Serve the mussels scattered with the coriander leaves and red chilli. **Serves 4**

You can make the paste a day in advance and store in the fridge until ready to use.

Roast fillet of beef with shallots and mushrooms

1½ hours + marinating, up to 24 hours

soy sauce 2 tbsp
red wine vinegar 1 tbsp
extra-virgin olive oil 6 tbsp
garlic 8 cloves, peeled: 4 crushed, 4 left whole
beef fillet 1, about 1.75kg
shallots 10 small, peeled
fresh rosemary 1 small bunch, stems removed
mixed mushrooms such as **chanterelle, oyster** and **chestnut** 350g, halved or quartered if large

For even cooking, try to buy an evenly shaped fillet. If it's not a uniform thickness, tuck the small ends under and tie with string or ask your butcher to do it. The longer you can marinate the meat, the more flavour it will take on.

■ Mix 1 tbsp soy, the vinegar and 3 tbsp olive oil with 4 garlic cloves, crushed. Season the beef with plenty of salt and put in a large plastic zip bag with the marinade. Marinate in the fridge for at least 1 hour and up to 24 hours.

■ Let the beef come to room temperature a couple of hours before roasting. Pat dry and season again. Heat the oven to 200C/fan 180C/gas 6. Heat 1 tbsp olive oil in a heavy-based frying pan and sear the beef well on all sides, then put it in a large roasting tin with the shallots. Sprinkle over half the rosemary and roast for 25 minutes for rare beef (give it another 10 minutes for medium-rare), cover with foil and a tea towel while you cook the mushrooms.

■ Mix the mushrooms with the remaining olive oil, soy sauce, garlic cloves and rosemary. Put the mix on a large shallow baking sheet, season and roast in the oven for 15 minutes. Slice the meat and serve with a spoonful of mushrooms and shallots. **Serves 8**

Trout koulibiac

45 minutes

skinless trout fillets 2
cooked rice 250g (100g uncooked will make
    this amount)
spring onions 2, finely sliced
eggs 3, 2 hard-boiled and chopped, 1 beaten,
    for glazing
lemon 1, zested and juiced
dill leaves chopped, 2 tbsp
puff pastry 500g block

■ Microwave the trout on a plate covered
with cling film for 3 minutes (or steam for
4 minutes). Flake into a bowl and mix with
the rice, onion, chopped egg, zest, juice and
dill. Season.

■ Heat the oven to 200C/fan 180C/gas 6.
Roll out the pastry to the thickness of a
£1 coin on a floured surface and divide in 2
(divide the pastry first if you are short on
space). Lift 1 piece on to a buttered baking
sheet, spoon the trout mix into the middle
and spread to a 10 x 18cm rectangle. Wet
a border around the filling, put the other
piece of pastry on top, press down around
the filling and trim the edges (use these for
decoration). Brush with glaze, cut slits in
the top and bake for 30 minutes. **Serves 4**

Koulibiac is a traditional Russian pie,
usually filled with salmon or sturgeon.
This version uses trout.

Roast goose with sour cherry and red wine sauce

30 minutes + 2–2½ hours in the oven

goose 1 oven ready, about 4.5kg
Maldon sea salt
onion 1, quartered
fresh rosemary 1 small bunch

SOUR CHERRY SAUCE
shallots 3, finely chopped
butter
dried sour cherries 50g
red wine ½ bottle
chicken stock 250ml
cinnamon stick 1
redcurrant jelly 3 tbsp

The size of an uncooked goose can be deceptive. A goose contains a lot of fat that will cook out, causing it to shrink in the oven.

■ Heat the oven to 220C/fan 200C/gas 7. Remove any excess fat from the goose cavity. Prick the goose all over with a fork (especially the really fatty bits) then rub with the sea salt flakes. Put the onion and rosemary in the cavity then sit the goose on a trivet in a large roasting tin. Cook for 30 minutes then turn the oven down to 180C/fan 160C/gas 4 and cook for another 1½–2 hours (drain off the excess fat a couple of times during cooking). To test if the goose is cooked, pierce the thick part of the thigh with a skewer – the juices should run clear. Leave to rest for 30 minutes before carving.

■ While the goose is resting, make the sauce. Fry the shallots in a knob of butter until softened. Add the rest of the ingredients (apart from the redcurrant jelly) and simmer until reduced and syrupy. Stir in the redcurrant jelly and another knob of butter until melted and glossy. Serve with the goose. **Serves 6**

Pumpkin and sage pot pies

1 hour

onion 1 small, cut into thin wedges
garlic 1 clove, finely chopped
pumpkin or **butternut squash** 400g, peeled, cut into chunks
sage leaves 1 small bunch, roughly torn
olive oil
dry white wine 5 tbsp
mascarpone 150g
vegetable stock 150ml
egg 1, beaten, for glazing

PASTRY
plain flour 150g
butter 75g, chilled and diced

To save time, use bought shortcrust for the pies. All-butter versions have a better flavour.

■ Heat the oven to 200C/fan 180C/gas 6. For the pastry, sift the flour and a pinch of salt into a large bowl. Rub in the butter with your fingers to form breadcrumbs. Stir in 4–5 tsp cold water to make a soft dough. Wrap in cling film and chill.

■ Put the onion, garlic, pumpkin/squash and sage in a large roasting tin. Season. Mix in 2 tbsp olive oil. Spread out in a single layer then roast for 30 minutes, stirring occasionally.

■ Sit the roasting tin on the hob over a medium heat and pour in the wine. Simmer until reduced by half, then stir in the mascarpone until melted. Stir in the vegetable stock and bring to a simmer. Remove from the heat.

■ Roll out the pastry and cut 2 discs slightly larger than the tops of 2 individual pie dishes. Divide the filling between the dishes and brush the rims with egg. Lay the pastry over the filling and crimp the edges. Brush the pastry with beaten egg and bake for 20–25 mins. **Serves 2**

Spiced autumn lamb with butternut squash purée

40 minutes + marinating

cumin seeds ½ tbsp

coriander seeds ½ tbsp

garlic 1 clove, crushed

olive oil

rack of lamb 2, each 6 bone, French
   trimmed

butternut squash or **pumpkin** 500g, peeled
   and chopped

butter

coriander leaves a small handful, chopped

■ Crush the spices using a pestle and mortar. Mix together with the garlic and a large slug of olive oil and some seasoning then rub all over the lamb. Leave to sit for 30 minutes.

■ Heat the oven to 200C/fan 180C/gas 6. Cook the lamb for 20 minutes for pink then leave to rest for 10 minutes.

■ Meanwhile steam the squash until tender then whiz in a food processor with a knob of butter and seasoning to make a purée. Stir in the coriander. Serve 3 cutlets, each with some purée and green veg or salad. **Serves 4**

Lamb is often thought of as springtime food but a few more months out in the pasture gives a fuller flavoured meat.

Mini toad-in-the-holes with Bramley gravy

1 hour

onions 2, sliced

olive oil

Bramley apple 1 large, peeled, cored and
    cubed

chicken stock 500ml

plain flour 150g

eggs 2

milk 300ml

rosemary needles, a few, finely chopped

pork chipolatas 12

■ Cook the onions with a little oil until dark golden brown and caramelized, at least 20–25 minutes. Add the apple and stock, and cook until the apple completely breaks down and thickens the gravy (use a spoon or masher to help). Season.

■ Whisk together the flour, eggs and milk with lots of seasoning then stir in the rosemary.

■ Heat the oven to 220C/fan 200/gas 7. Brown the chipolatas then put 3 in the bottom of each of 4 ovenproof dishes with 1 tbsp oil. Heat in the oven for 5 minutes then pour in the batter and cook for 25–30 minutes until puffed and golden.

■ Serve with the gravy. **Serves 4**

Don't be tempted to use other apples for this. Bramleys will break down completely when cooked to give you a lovely appley gravy to go with your bangers.

Shallot tarte Tatin

1 hour

butter 50g
shallots 500g, peeled
balsamic vinegar 4 tbsp
demerara sugar 3 tbsp
thyme leaves from 3 sprigs
all-butter puff pastry 500g block

■ Heat the butter in an ovenproof pan that the shallots will fit in an even layer. Add the shallots and cook over a medium heat until they start to brown. Add the balsamic and sugar and a cup of water. Keep cooking, adding more water if you need to until the shallots are completely cooked through and the balsamic and sugar has become sticky and caramelized around them. Mix in the thyme leaves. Season.

■ Heat the oven to 200C/fan 180C/gas 6. Roll out the pastry to the thickness of a 20p coin. Cut a circle a little larger than the pan then lay it over the shallots and tuck down the sides. Put in the oven for 20–25 minutes until the pastry is puffed, golden and crisp. Invert on to a plate and serve in wedges.

Serves 4

Serve with a wedge of blue cheese and a crisp salad for a smart vegetarian lunch.

Baked risotto with lemon, courgettes and basil

40 minutes

olive oil 4 tbsp

onion 1, chopped

garlic 1 clove, chopped

courgettes 500g, sliced

arborio rice 500g

vegetable stock 1.2 litres, hot

lemons 2, zested and juiced

Grana Padano or Parmesan 100g, freshly
    grated

basil leaves 1 small bunch, roughly chopped,
    to garnish

■ Heat the oven to 180C/fan 160C/gas 4. Heat the oil in an overproof dish with a lid and fry the onion and garlic for 5 minutes. Stir in the courgettes and rice, coating everything in oil and cook for a few more minutes. Add the stock, lemon juice and cheese, cover and bake in the oven for 30 minutes.

■ Serve sprinkled with the lemon zest and basil. **Serves 12**

Grana Padano costs less than Parmesan but works just as well in Italian dishes.

Pea, tarragon and cream cheese pithivier

50 minutes + chilling

puff pastry 1 x 500g block
onion 1, finely chopped
butter
frozen peas 150g, defrosted
soft cheese 125g, beaten until soft
tarragon leaves small bunch, chopped
parsley leaves a handful, chopped
lemon ½, zested
egg 1, beaten

■ Roll out the pastry and cut into 2 x 14cm circles and 2 x 16cm circles
■ Cook the onion in a knob of butter until softened. Cool and mix with the peas, cheese, tarragon, parsley and lemon.
■ Heat the oven to 200C/fan 180C/gas 6. Lay the 2 smaller pastry circles out on a baking sheet and heap the filling in the middle, brush around the edges with egg and lay the bigger circles on top. Press the edges together with a fork, score a pattern on the top and brush with egg. Bake for 25 minutes or until puffed and golden.
Makes 2

To defrost peas quickly, put in a colander and pour over a kettle of boiling water.

Linguine with clams, chilli and garlic

20 minutes

clams 800g, cleaned

linguine 300g

olive oil

garlic 2 cloves, sliced

red chilli 2, finely sliced

white wine a glass

parsley leaves 1 small bunch, chopped

■ Check the clams – if any are open, give them a tap on the work surface – if they don't close, throw them away. Cook the pasta according to packet instructions.

■ Heat a really good slug of olive oil in a large shallow pan with a lid. Add the garlic and chilli and sizzle for a couple of minutes. Tip in the clams and wine, put on the lid and leave for a few minutes until all the clams are open (throw away any that stay closed).

■ Drain the pasta and tip into the clam pan with the parsley. Toss everything together and serve. **Serves 4**

Ask your fishmonger for small, sweet palourde (also called carpet-shell) clams, either sustainably harvested or farmed off the south coast.

Roasted tomato and Parmesan tart

1 hour

small vine tomatoes 8–10, halved
olive oil
puff pastry 500g block
Parmesan or **Grana Padano** 50g, roughly grated
Dijon mustard 1 tbsp
mascarpone 2 tbsp
garlic 2 cloves, sliced
thyme leaves from 2 sprigs, chopped
egg 1, beaten to glaze

■ Heat the oven to 200C/fan 180C/gas 6. Season the tomatoes, drizzle with oil then put cut-side down on a non-stick baking sheet. Roast for 10 minutes. Cool and slip off the skins.

■ Roll out the pastry to the thickness of a £1 coin. Sprinkle with half the cheese, fold in half, then roll out to the same thickness. Sprinkle over the rest of the cheese and roll out again. Using a dinner plate as a guide, cut out a large circle (about 28cm). Score a border about 1 ½ cm in from the edge.

■ Mix together the mustard and mascarpone and spread inside the border. Arrange the tomato halves cut-side up inside the border. Season and sprinkle with garlic, thyme and olive oil. Glaze the edges then bake for 30–40 minutes until the pastry is crisp and golden. **Serves 6**

You can add all sorts of sweet and savoury flavours to bought puff pastry using this method – try herbs in a savoury or cinnamon in a sweet pastry.

Golden chicken pilaff

50 minutes

---

butter 50g
chicken breasts 4 skinless, cut into chunks
onions 2, halved and sliced
garlic 3 cloves, sliced
cinnamon stick 1
cardamom pods 5, lightly bruised
cloves 4 whole
chicken stock 500ml and mixed with a
    large pinch of **saffron**
basmati rice 300g
coriander leaves a handful, roughly
    chopped, to garnish

■ Heat half the butter in a large, wide pan with a lid. Brown the chicken pieces all over in batches and remove. Add the rest of the butter then tip in the onions and cook really slowly until meltingly tender and golden brown (about 10 minutes).

■ Add the garlic and cook for 2 minutes. Add the cinnamon, cardamom pods and cloves, and cook for a minute. Add the chicken stock and chicken pieces and stir. Pour in the rice and stir well.

■ Cover tightly (if the lid isn't really secure, put a sheet of foil underneath) and cook on a really gentle heat for a further 15–20 minutes until all the liquid has been absorbed and the rice is tender. Scatter the coriander over and serve. **Serves 4**

This tastes just as good using chicken thigh fillets. You'll need 8 skinless fillets for this recipe.

Herb and polenta crusted lamb

15 minutes

lamb cutlets 6, fat trimmed off

plain flour 4 tbsp, seasoned

egg 1, beaten

instant polenta 6 tbsp, mixed with 1 tbsp
    finely chopped rosemary

olive oil for frying and to serve

watercress to serve

lemon wedges plus squeeze of juice, to
    serve

■ Dip each lamb cutlet into the flour, then in the egg then the polenta herb mix. Heat a shallow layer of olive oil in a frying pan and fry for 2–3 minutes each side until crisp and light golden. Serve the cutlets with watercress dressed with a little more olive oil and lemon juice, and lemon wedges.

Serves 2

Instant polenta is much finer than normal and will give you a crisper crust.

Red mullet escabèche

20 minutes

red mullet 4 fillets, skin on and scaled
oil

MARINADE
red onion 1 small, sliced
red chilli 1, finely shredded
bay leaf 1
coriander seeds ½ tbsp, lightly crushed
white wine vinegar 1 tbsp
white wine 1 small glass

■ Heat together all the marinade ingredients until hot.

■ Fry the red mullet fillets for 2 minutes each side in a little oil.

■ Put in a baking dish in a snug single layer and pour over the marinade. Leave to cool and serve at room temperature. (It will keep in the fridge for 1–2 days.) **Serves 4**

Escabèche is a dish of fish or meat that has been cooked then marinated and served cold or at room temperature. Variations can be found in Spanish, Peruvian and Provençal cuisines.

BBQ tamarind salmon with lemon grass, chilli and ginger

25 minutes

tamarind purée 100g jar
lemon grass 2 stalks, sliced (woody layers removed)
red chilli 1 small, seeded and finely chopped
root ginger 3cm, grated
palm sugar or **honey** 3 tbsp
mint leaves 1 small bunch, chopped
salmon 700g piece, skin on
coriander leaves a small handful, chopped, to garnish

■ Mix the tamarind, lemon grass, chilli, ginger, palm sugar and mint together in a small bowl. Put the salmon on a greased piece of foil or a banana leaf (find these in the frozen section at Asian supermarkets).
■ Brush a thick layer of the sauce over the salmon and grill for 10 minutes.
■ Serve sprinkled with coriander and a bowl of extra marinade on the side for dipping. **Serves 6**

Find small jars of tamarind purée in the spice or Asian section of most major supermarkets.

Chicken with wine, tarragon and green beans

30 minutes

olive oil

chicken breasts 4, skin on

shallots 2, finely sliced

white wine 300ml

butter 100g, cold, diced

tarragon leaves from 1 small bunch

green beans 300g, blanched for 2 minutes
   and drained

■ Heat a little oil in a large non-stick frying pan. Season the chicken breasts then cook skin-side down until the skin is crisp and golden brown. Turn over and continue to cook until the chicken is just done, about 8 minutes, remove and keep warm in a low oven.

■ Add the shallots to the chicken pan and cook until softened. Add the wine then bubble until reduced by half.

■ Whisk in the butter then stir through the tarragon and beans, and season. Serve the chicken with the beans. **Serves 4**

Tarragon can vary quite widely in strength, so taste a little before you add it.

Glazed hoisin duck

25 minutes

hoisin sauce 4 tbsp

Chinese five-spice 1 tsp

duck breasts 2 skin on

oil

sesame seeds 2 tbsp

green pepper 1, seeded and cut into thin strips

spring onions 3, shredded

carrots 2, cut into thin strips (use a peeler)

sesame oil 2 tbsp

■ Mix the hoisin sauce and five-spice in a bowl. Score the duck skin diagonally and marinate the breast in the sauce for 10 minutes.

■ Heat a little oil to hot in a non-stick pan. Shake the excess marinade from the duck then put in the pan skin-side down and cook for 5–7 minutes until the skin turns crisp. Turn the heat down to medium, turn the duck over and brush with the remaining marinade until cooked, about 10 minutes.

■ Meanwhile, lightly toast the sesame seeds in a frying pan. Mix the vegetables with the sesame seeds and sesame oil.

■ Serve the duck breast with the salad.

Serves 2

Scoring the duck breast allows more of the fat to escape and crisps up the skin.

Artichoke and bacon tart

1 hour 15 minutes

ready-rolled shortcrust pastry 375g
bacon rashers 6, chopped
onion 1 small, sliced
butter
cooked artichoke hearts 6, halved
eggs 4
double cream 100ml
Parmesan 50g, freshly grated
flat-leaf parsley leaves a small handful,
    chopped

■ Heat the oven to 190C/fan 170C/gas 5. Use the pastry to line a 24cm tart tin. Blind bake for 10–15 minutes and cool.

■ Turn the oven down to 180C/fan 160C/gas 4. Meanwhile, cook the bacon and onion in a little butter until softened then put in the pastry case with the artichoke.

■ Whisk the eggs, cream and 30g Parmesan together, add the parsley, season well and pour over the filling. Sprinkle the remaining parmesan over the top. Bake for 25–30 minutes or until just set. Serve warm. **Serves 4**

Buy cooked, prepared artichoke hearts in cans or in olive oil in jars. Avoid ones with too many added flavourings for this tart.

Pork loin with apricot, sage and pine nut stuffing

2½ hours

butter

celery 2 sticks, diced

onion 1 medium, chopped

sage leaves chopped, 3 tbsp

thyme leaves chopped, 2 tbsp

French bread 30g, cubed

pine nuts 30g

dried whole apricots 10, chopped

boned pork loin 2kg, butterflied flat

■ Heat the oven to 180C/fan 160C/gas 4. Melt a knob of butter in a frying pan then add the celery, onion, 1 tbsp sage and 1 tbsp thyme. Season and cook until soft, about 5 minutes. Tip the bread, pine nuts and apricots into a bowl and pour over the onion mixture. Season again and mix well. Lay the meat out flat and spread the stuffing over it. Roll up and tie with string.

■ Sprinkle the outside of the joint with the remaining thyme, sage and some seasoning. Put in a roasting tin and roast for 2 hours. Leave to rest for 20 minutes, remove string then cut into thick slices.

Serves 6

Get your butcher to score the skin really well for the best crackling.

Pear and dolcelatte tarts

50 minutes

ready-rolled puff pastry 500g block
dolcelatte 75g
mascarpone 4 tbsp
pears 2, peeled, halved, cored and sliced
egg 1, beaten to glaze
pine nuts 3 tbsp
thyme leaves from 2 sprigs
clear honey for drizzling

■ Heat the oven to 200C/fan 180C/gas 6. Roll out the pastry then cut into 4 circles about 14cm in diameter and score a border about a finger's-width in from the edge.

■ Mash together the dolcelatte and mascarpone and dot inside the border. Arrange slices of pear on top and glaze the border with egg. Cook for 15 minutes then scatter with the pine nuts and thyme and cook for another 5–10 minutes until puffed and golden. Drizzle with a little honey before serving. **Serves 4**

Dolcelatte is a lovely, creamy blue cheese but you could also use a Gorgonzola or a creamy Stilton here instead.

Piri-piri guinea fowl

1 hour + marinating

guinea fowl 2, spatchcocked

PIRI-PIRI MARINADE
red chillies 4, finely chopped
limes 2, juiced
garlic 3 cloves, crushed
ground coriander 1 tsp
ground cinnamon 1 tsp
ground ginger 1 tsp
parsley leaves 1 small bunch, chopped
salad or sauté to serve

■ Put the guinea fowl in a shallow dish, mix together the marinade ingredients and pour over. Chill for a couple of hours, or overnight if possible.

■ Heat the oven to 200C/fan 180C/gas 6. Put the birds in a roasting tin skin-side up and pour over the marinade.

■ Cook for about 45 minutes (basting occasionally with the marinade) until crisp, golden and cooked through. Chop into quarters (leave on the bone) and serve with salad or sauté potatoes. **Serves 4**

Guinea fowl has a more gamey flavour than chicken, so it stands up to strong marinades really well.

Tomato and tarragon tarte Tatin

20 minutes + 2½ hours in the oven

tomatoes 8, cut in half
tarragon leaves 2 tbsp, roughly chopped, plus a few whole leaves to serve
unsalted butter 50g
balsamic vinegar 1 tbsp
ready-rolled puff pastry 375g

■ Heat the oven to 160C/fan 140C/gas 3. Arrange the tomatoes cut-side up on a wire rack set over a roasting tin. Sprinkle with sea salt and scatter over the tarragon leaves. Put in the oven for 2 hours, until semi-dried.

■ Remove from the oven and increase the temperature to 200C/fan 180C/gas 6.

■ Divide the butter between 2 ovenproof frying pans (about 18cm each) or 1 large one and put over a medium heat. When the butter foams, stir in the balsamic vinegar and season.

■ Divide the tomatoes between the frying pans, arranging them cut-side down in a single layer. Remove from the heat. Cut 2 circles of pastry large enough to cover the tomatoes then lay them over the top, pushing down gently. Bake for 20–30 minutes until the pastry is puffed up and golden. Carefully invert the tarts on to plates, sprinkle with tarragon leaves and serve. **Serves 2**

Leave the tarts in the pan for 5 minutes before turning out to let them settle.

Roasted squash with chilli and sage crumbs

45 minutes

butternut squash 2, cut into thin wedges, seeded
fresh breadcrumbs 80g
olive oil
garlic 2 cloves, sliced
red chilli 1, sliced
sage leaves 1 small bunch
Grana Padano 3 tbsp, freshly grated

■ Heat the oven to 200C/fan 180C/gas 6. Put the squash in a baking dish. Toss the breadcrumbs with 2 tbsp oil and season. Sprinkle the squash with the garlic, chilli and sage, drizzle with 2 tbsp oil, season and sprinkle with the breadcrumbs and cheese. Bake for 35–40 minutes until tender and golden. **Serves 12**

To make fresh breadcrumbs quickly whiz broken-up bread in a food processor.

Antipasti salad

15 minutes

mixed salad leaves 200g (2 bags)
artichoke hearts 100g jar, drained
Peppadews sweet peppers 50g, drained
celery ½, sliced
red onion 1 small, sliced

DRESSING
red wine vinegar 2 tbsp
extra-virgin olive oil 3 tbsp
garlic ½ clove, crushed
Dijon mustard ½ tsp
caster sugar ½ tsp

■ Put the salad leaves, artichoke hearts, Peppadews, celery and onion in a bowl. Add the dressing ingredients to a glass jar with a fitted lid, season and shake well. Pour over the salad just before serving and toss.
Serves 6

Peppadews (sweet pickled peppers, available in jars and delis) add heat and crunch to this salad.

Radicchio with caper and balsamic sauce

20 minutes

radicchio 2

olive oil

chicken or vegetable stock 100ml

butter 15g

capers 2 tbsp, rinsed and drained

shallots 3, finely sliced

balsamic vinegar 4 tbsp (a good quality one)

parsley leaves a good handful, chopped

■ Quarter the radicchio and lay them cut-side up in a baking dish. Brush with a little oil, pour in the stock and grill under a medium heat for 10 minutes or until the radicchio is tender.

■ Heat the butter in a frying pan and add the capers and shallots, fry briefly, then stir in the balsamic and bubble together, then add the parsley. Pour this over the radicchio. Serve with roast or grilled meat or slices of grilled sourdough. **Serves 4**

Long radicchio, called Treviso, has a milder flavour than the round, cabbage-shaped variety and cooks particularly well.

Peas with baby leeks, prosciutto and tarragon

30 minutes

baby leeks 8, trimmed, or use baby onions
or small shallots, 16, peeled
butter
chicken stock 200ml
frozen peas 500g
double cream 142ml carton
tarragon leaves chopped, 2 tbsp
prosciutto 6 slices, grilled until crisp

■ Cook the leeks or onions in a large, wide pan with a knob of butter and a little seasoning for about 5 minutes until just starting to colour. Add the stock, cover and simmer until leeks are tender and the stock has reduced. Add the peas, cream and tarragon, and simmer uncovered until the peas are cooked. Serve scattered with the crisp prosciutto. **Serves 4**

For vegetarian guests, replace the chicken stock with vegetable stock and leave out the prosciutto.

Perfect goose-fat roasties

1 hour 20 minutes

goose or **duck fat** 6 tbsp
potatoes 2kg, peeled and cut to a similar size (King Edward or Maris Piper are good)
rosemary needles from 2 sprigs (optional)
Maldon sea salt

■ Heat the oven to 200C/fan 180C/gas 6. Put the fat in a roasting tin in the oven to heat. Drop the potatoes into a pan of boiling water and cook for 5 minutes, then drain really well in a colander. Shake the potatoes around in the colander to rough up the edges a bit then carefully tip them into the hot fat, turning them over to coat. Put back in the oven for about 50 minutes or until crisp and golden. Turn them halfway through and add the rosemary (if using). Drain on kitchen paper and sprinkle with salt before serving. **Serves 8**

Invest in a solid, non-stick shallow roasting tin. Cheaper ones buckle, and you won't get an even distribution of fat to cook your roasties.

Parsnip and potato rösti

40 minutes

potato 200g, peeled and grated
parsnips 200g small, peeled and grated
onion ½, grated
thyme leaves from 2 sprigs
butter 25g, melted, plus extra for frying

■ Put the grated potato in a clean tea towel and squeeze to remove excess water. Tip into a bowl with the parsnip, onion, thyme and melted butter. Season really well and mix.

■ Heat a non-stick frying pan to hot then tip in the mixture and press down with a spatula. Cook for 6–8 minutes until golden brown and crisp underneath. Flip the rösti out on to a plate then put back in raw-side down and continue cooking for another 6–8 minutes until completely cooked through.

■ Divide into 2 and serve. **Serves 2**

You shouldn't have to remove the woody cores from parsnips when they are really young, but as they get older it's best to cut them out.

Waldorf salad

20 minutes

apples 2 red skinned, such as Cox's or
    Braeburn
lemon ½, juiced
mayonnaise 4 tbsp
Dijon mustard 1 tbsp
celery 2 sticks, cut into chunks
walnut halves a handful
watercress a couple of handfuls

■ Cut the apple into chunks and toss with
the lemon juice.

■ Mix together the mayonnaise and
mustard, and toss with all the other
ingredients. **Serves 2**

**If you want to upgrade this to a main meal,
add some cooked, shredded chicken.**

Turnip gratin with cider, cream and bacon

50 minutes

---

double cream 284ml carton
cider 100ml
Dijon mustard 1 tbsp
young turnips 750g, peeled and sliced
rindless back bacon rashers 6, cut into
  small pieces

■ Heat the oven to 200C/fan 180C/gas 6. Put the cream and cider into a large pan and simmer for a couple of minutes.

■ Season then add the mustard and turnip slices and cook for 5 minutes. Fry the bacon until crisp. Tip the turnip mix and bacon into a gratin dish, leaving some bacon for the top. Cook for 25–30 minutes until golden and bubbling. **Serves 4**

Use a dry-ish cider for best results.

Broccoli with anchovies, capers and chilli

15 minutes

broccoli 1 head, cut into florets

olive oil

anchovies 2, chopped

capers 1 tbsp, rinsed and drained

red chilli 2, finely chopped

garlic 2 cloves, finely chopped

ciabatta 3 slices, crusts cut off and chopped into rough, chunky breadcrumbs

■ Steam the broccoli florets for 3–4 minutes until just tender.

■ Heat 2 tbsp olive oil in a pan and add the anchovies, capers, chilli and half the garlic. Cook on a gentle heat for 2–3 minutes. Heat another 2 tbsp oil in a frying pan then add the chunky breadcrumbs and rest of garlic, and cook until crisp, crunchy and golden, then drain on kitchen paper.

■ Toss the broccoli with the flavoured oil, tip into a dish then scatter over breadcrumbs and serve. **Serves 4**

The anchovies in this dish just give a salty rather than fishy flavour.

Marinated red onion, spinach and pine nut salad

25 minutes

---

red onion 1, halved and sliced
caster sugar 1 tbsp
red wine vinegar 2 tbsp
young leaf spinach 100g
pine nuts 4 tbsp, toasted
olive oil
cumin seeds 1 tsp
natural yoghurt 150ml

■ Put the red onions in a bowl and toss with the sugar and vinegar. Leave for 10–15 minutes to soften. Put the spinach in a large serving dish. Drain the onions then scatter over the spinach with the pine nuts.

■ Heat 2 tbsp olive oil and add the cumin seeds. When they start to pop, take off the heat and stir into the yoghurt. Drizzle over the salad and serve. **Serves 4**

Marinating the onions gives them a lovely sweet and sour flavour, and takes away some of the rawness.

Cucumber with soured cream and dill

25 minutes

cucumber 1, halved lengthways, seeded
    then thickly sliced on the diagonal
sea salt flakes 1 tsp
red onion 1, halved and finely sliced
soured cream 142ml carton
dill 1 small bunch, finely chopped, reserve a
    little to garnish (optional)
horseradish cream or sauce 1 tbsp

■ Put the cucumber in a colander over a large bowl. Sprinkle with the salt and leave for 20 minutes. Put the cucumber in a bowl, add the onion, soured cream, dill and horseradish, then season with black pepper. Toss everything together and serve sprinkled with a little more dill, if you like.

Serves 4

Salting the cucumber gets rid of a lot of the liquid and makes it really crunchy.

Runner beans with tomato, garlic and chilli

40 minutes

runner beans 300g
olive oil 3 tbsp
garlic 2 cloves, finely sliced
dried chilli flakes a large pinch
cloves 2
plum tomatoes 2 x 400g cans, drained of
    juice
basil leaves 1 small bunch, torn

■ Run a potato peeler down either side of the beans to remove any stringy bits. Cut on the diagonal into 2cm pieces.
■ Heat the olive oil in a large, wide frying pan and add the garlic. Cook for 2 minutes then add the beans, chilli and cloves. Cook for 2 minutes then tip in the drained tomatoes. Cover and cook for 20–30 minutes until the beans are tender and the sauce is thick and rich. Stir through the basil just before serving. **Serves 4**

Runner beans can be cooked briefly so they still have a little bite or slowly stewed in a sauce until really tender.

Bulgar wheat, feta and herb salad

15 minutes

bulgar wheat 150g

ground cumin 1½ tsp

feta 100g

cherry tomatoes 100g, quartered

basil leaves a handful

fresh chives snipped, 2 tbsp

extra-virgin olive oil

lime ½, juiced

■ Put the bulgar wheat in a bowl with the cumin and just cover with boiling water. Set aside for 10 minutes to soften and absorb the liquid. Drain off any excess.

■ Meanwhile, crumble the feta into a bowl with the tomatoes and herbs. Add to the bulgar wheat and mix together. Divide between 2 plates and drizzle with a little oil and a squeeze of lime juice. **Serves 2**

Bulgar wheat is partly cooked cracked wheat, which needs soaking until it becomes tender.

New potatoes cooked in a bag with herb butter

50 minutes

butter 250g, softened
parsley, tarragon, basil and **chervil** 1 bunch
(use one or a mixture)
garlic 2 cloves, crushed
lemon 1, zested
baby new potatoes 500g

■ Put the butter, herbs, garlic and lemon in a food processor and season well. Whiz until combined then put on a sheet of cling film and twist into a sausage shape. Wrap in foil and freeze. The butter will keep in the freezer for a few weeks – just cut slices to use when you need them.

■ Heat the oven to 180C/fan 160C/gas 4. Take 4 lengths of baking parchment. Put a quarter of the potatoes on each sheet of parchment. Top with a couple of slices of the herb butter. Fold over the parchment and turn in the edges to make a parcel. Repeat for the other 3 parcels. Put on a baking sheet and cook for 30–40 minutes. Serve in the bag. **Serves 4**

Cooking these potatoes in a bag infuses them with all the herby, buttery flavours.

Baked Parmesan courgettes

1 hour 10 minutes

courgettes 8 small, halved lengthways
plum tomatoes 4, chopped
garlic 2 cloves, crushed
chilli 1, seeded and finely chopped
rosemary needles 1 tsp finely, chopped
olive oil
breadcrumbs 4 tbsp, mixed with 6 tbsp
    freshly grated **Parmesan**

■ Heat the oven to 200C/fan 180C/gas 6. Scoop the seeds from the middle of each courgette half with a teaspoon so that you have 16 'boats'. Put in 1 large or 2 smaller ovenproof dishes and season. Mix together the tomatoes, garlic, chilli and rosemary with a slug of olive oil and season.
■ Pile the mixture into the courgettes then cover the dishes with foil. Bake for 30 minutes or until tender, then remove the foil and scatter over the breadcrumb mix. Drizzle with olive oil and bake for another 20 minutes until golden and crisp. **Serves 4**

Use small or baby courgettes for this as they have less water and bake more easily.

Indian-spiced green beans

15 minutes

green beans 300g
groundnut oil 2 tbsp
root ginger thumb-sized piece, sliced into
    long, thin strips
garlic 1 clove, finely chopped
dried chilli flakes a pinch
black mustard seeds 2 tsp

■ Blanch the beans for 2 minutes in boiling water then rinse in cold water and drain. Heat the oil and cook the ginger and garlic for 2 minutes – don't let it burn. Turn up the heat a little, add the chilli and mustard seeds, then stir until the seeds start to pop. Add the beans and warm through. **Serves 4**

Green beans are the perfect foil for spices – they only need briefly cooking as it's good to serve them with a little bit of bite.

Potato gratins with garlic and Red Leicester

1 hour

butter for greasing
Maris Piper or **King Edward potatoes** 5
    large, about 1.2kg, cut into 2cm chunks
garlic 1 clove, chopped
onion 1, chopped
olive oil 2 tbsp
crème fraîche 150ml
milk 125ml
Red Leicester 200g, freshly grated
Parmesan 30g, freshly grated

■ Heat the oven to 160C/fan 140C/gas 3. Butter 6 ramekins or 1 large baking dish.
■ Boil the potatoes in salted water until just tender, drain. Fry the garlic and onion in a little olive oil for 5 minutes until soft.
■ Mix the crème fraîche and milk together in a large bowl then stir in the potatoes, onion mix and both cheeses. Pour into the ramekins or baking dish, and cook in the oven for 45–50 minutes until golden and bubbling. Leave for 10 minutes before serving. **Makes 6**

Using Red Leicester gives these gratins a sharp flavour and brilliant orange colour.

Lamb's lettuce, orange and roast beet salad

1 hour

beetroot 4, golf-ball sized
olive oil
cumin seeds ½ tsp
lamb's lettuce 100g
oranges 2, segmented
red onion ½, sliced

DRESSING
olive oil 3 tbsp
red wine vinegar 1 tbsp
fresh orange juice 1 tbsp
wholegrain mustard 2 tsp

■ Heat the oven to 200C/fan 180C/gas 6. Toss the beets in a little olive oil with the cumin and roast until tender, about 40–50 minutes. Cool, peel and cut into wedges.

■ Arrange the lamb's lettuce, beets, orange segments and onion on a platter. Whisk together the dressing ingredients and pour over. **Serves 4**

You can use cooked beetroot in this salad if you want to save time. Just add ½ tsp of toasted cumin seeds to the dressing.

Sweet potato gratin

1 hour

double cream 284ml carton
whole nutmeg a good grating
dried chilli flakes a pinch
garlic 1 clove, crushed
fresh rosemary 2 sprigs, needles stripped
    off and chopped
sweet potatoes 1kg, peeled and sliced

■ Heat the oven to 190C/fan 170C/gas 5.
Put all the ingredients except the sweet
potatoes in a small pan, season really
well and bring to just below boiling point.
Arrange the sweet potato slices in a
shallow ovenproof dish and pour over the
infused cream. Bake for 30–40 minutes
until the potato is tender and the top
golden and bubbling. **Serves 4**

Try to always use whole nutmeg. It keeps
longer and you can just grate some when
you need it.

Roasted butternut squash salad with soy-balsamic dressing

25 minutes

butternut squash 1kg, peeled and cut into 2cm cubes
olive oil
Puy lentils 100g
rocket 100g
sesame seeds 1 tsp, toasted, to garnish
spring onions 6, sliced, to garnish

SOY DRESSING
olive oil 5 tbsp
balsamic vinegar 3 tbsp
soy sauce 1 tbsp
red chilli 1, seeded and chopped
garlic 1 clove, finely chopped
clear honey 1 tsp

■ Heat the oven to 200C/fan 180C/gas 6. Put the squash on a baking sheet, drizzle with 1 tbsp olive oil and season. Roast for 20 minutes or until tender, shaking the tray a couple of times to keep it from sticking.

■ Simmer the lentils for about 15 minutes or until al dente, then drain. Whisk together the dressing ingredients. Put the rocket in a shallow serving bowl and arrange the lentils and squash on top. Pour over the dressing and top with sesame seeds and spring onions. **Serves 4**

You can leave the squash unpeeled if you like as the skin is edible and becomes tender when roasted.

Spinach and quail's egg salad with sweet and sour dressing

20 minutes

quail's eggs 12
sourdough or **ciabatta** 2 slices, cubed into 2cm croutons
olive oil
green salad leaves or **baby spinach** 160g
red onion 1 small, sliced into rings

SWEET AND SOUR DRESSING
pancetta 4 slices, chopped
extra-virgin olive oil 5 tbsp
garlic 2 cloves, finely chopped
caster sugar 1 tbsp
cider vinegar 3 tbsp
fresh lemon juice 2 tbsp

■ Heat the oven to 200C/fan 180C/gas 6. Simmer the quail's eggs in boiling water for 2½ minutes then run under cold water to cool.

■ Spread the croutons on to a baking sheet. Drizzle over 1 tbsp of olive oil and season. Bake for 5 minutes or until golden and crisp, then cool.

■ To make the dressing, cook the pancetta without any oil in a small frying pan until crisp then drain on kitchen paper. Add the olive oil and garlic to the pan. Cook until lightly golden, then take off the heat and add the pancetta, sugar, vinegar, lemon juice and season. Put back on the heat and whisk together.

■ Arrange the salad or spinach leaves in bowls. Peel and halve the eggs and add them to the salad along with the onion and croutons. Pour the warm dressing over the top and toss well. **Serves 4**

If you can't get pancetta just use thin-cut unsmoked bacon instead.

Chicory braised with bacon, cider and garlic

30 minutes

butter
smoked streaky bacon rashers 8, chopped
garlic 1 fat clove, thinly sliced
chicory 4 heads, halved lengthways
cider 200ml

■ Melt a knob of butter in a large frying pan with a lid and cook the bacon until it starts to go golden at the edges. Add the garlic and cook briefly then scoop everything out.

■ Add the chicory to the pan cut-side down (with a bit more butter if needed) and cook until it gets a really good caramelized colour. Turn the chicory over; add back the bacon and garlic with the cider and bring to the boil. Put the lid on and simmer for 12–15 minutes or until tender. **Serves 4**

This dish would be great served with roast chicken and mash. The chicory takes on all the flavours of the smoked bacon and cider while cooking.

Lime and coconut angel cakes with passion fruit

1 hour 30 minutes

eggs 7 whites
lime 1, zested, plus 2 tsp juice
cream of tartar ¾ tsp (look in the baking section of supermarkets)
caster sugar 120g
plain flour 60g
cornflour 15g
desiccated coconut 50g
passion fruit 4 large

You can give these little cakes extra zing by finishing with candied lime zest. Simmer shredded zest in a syrup made from equal amounts of sugar and water then scoop out and cool – sprinkle over to finish.

■ Heat the oven to 160C/fan 140C/gas 3. Whisk the egg whites with a pinch of salt and the lime juice until foamy. Add the cream of tartar and continue to whisk until stiff but not dry. Gradually whisk in 90g caster sugar with the lime zest until it forms a thick and glossy meringue.

■ Sift the remaining caster sugar and the flours into a bowl, and fold into the meringue in 3 batches to retain as much air as possible. Fold in the desiccated coconut. Spoon into 6 unoiled 10cm bundt tins and bake for 30 minutes, until firm and pale golden on top.

■ Turn the tins upside down on a wire rack (this creates steam to loosen the cakes) and leave for 10 minutes. Give each cake a very firm shake and a tap to release them then cool completely on the wire rack.

■ Scoop out the passion fruit pulp and push through a sieve to remove the seeds. Drizzle the juice over the finished cakes before serving. **Makes 6**

Chocolate affogato

10 minutes

chocolate ice cream 500g carton
Baileys Irish Cream 200ml
espresso 4 shots, or strongly brewed coffee
   200ml, hot

■ Put 2–3 scoops of ice cream in the bottom of each of 4 small bowls or coffee cups. Pour 50ml Baileys over each followed by a shot of espresso. **Serves 4**

Don't like Baileys? Try Tia Maria, Frangelico or Amaretto instead.

White chocolate mousse with crushed Mini Eggs

20 minutes + chilling

white chocolate 200g
crème fraîche 200ml
double cream 200ml
Cadbury Mini Eggs crushed, to decorate

■ Melt the chocolate in a heatproof bowl set over, not in, a pan of boiling water. Take off the heat and cool a little. Stir in the crème fraîche and cream, and mix together until velvety smooth. Pour into 6 little glasses and chill for an hour.

■ Scatter over the crushed Mini Eggs just before serving. **Serves 6**

Be very gentle with the heat when melting as white chocolate can seize easily.

Spiced pineapple Tatins

45 minutes

puff pastry 500g block, rolled out to the
thickness of a £1 coin

pineapple 1 small, peeled and sliced into 6 x
2cm-thick rings

caster sugar 70g

unsalted butter 35g

star anise 1, ground using a pestle and
mortar

ground cinnamon ½ tsp

crème fraîche to serve (optional)

■ Cut 6 circles of pastry (about 10cm) to fit
mini tart tins. Chill.

■ Line the tins with baking parchment.
Heat the oven to 180C/fan 160C/gas 4. Core
the pineapple.

■ Heat the sugar gently in a pan until it
turns a light caramel colour – shake the
pan while it melts but don't stir or it will
crystallize. Take off the heat and stir in the
butter, star anise and cinnamon. Divide
among tins, put a slice of pineapple on
each and bake for 10 minutes.

■ Top each with a pastry circle, prick with
a fork and bake for 20 minutes. Cool for
5 minutes only, turn out and serve. **Serves 6**

You can make these ahead up until the last
stage then cook the pastry before dinner.

Champagne syllabub

10 minutes

double cream 284ml carton
icing sugar 4 tbsp
Champagne 200ml

■ Whip the cream and sugar together to form soft peaks then whip in the Champagne until you have a soft, spoonable mixture. **Serves 4**

Serve this with pastel-coloured macaroons from delis or patisseries.

Pink rhubarb pavlova

2 hours + cooling

rhubarb 300g, cut into 4cm lengths (you want the forced, really pink stuff)

caster sugar 100g

grenadine 2 tbsp

double cream 568ml carton, softly whipped

MERINGUE

eggs 4 whites

golden caster 200g

cornflour 1 tsp

white wine vinegar 1 tsp

■ Heat the oven to 180C/fan 160C/gas 4. To make the meringue, whisk the egg whites to stiff peaks, then add the sugar a bit at a time, whisking until glossy and stiff. Whisk in the cornflour and vinegar.

■ Use a dinner plate to trace a circle on a piece of baking parchment then fill with the meringue and use a large palette knife to draw up the edges. Turn the oven down to 120C/fan 100C/gas ½. Cook for 1½ hours then take from oven and leave to cool completely.

■ Cook the rhubarb and sugar in a large pan, with a splash of water, on a low heat until tender. Put the grenadine in a separate pan and reduce to a syrup. Cool and mix with the rhubarb. To serve, pile the cream on top of the pavlova, top with the rhubarb and a drizzle of syrup. **Serves 8**

Grenadine gives the rhubarb a vivid pink colour.

Frozen lemon and ginger yoghurt terrine

30 minutes + freezing

Greek yoghurt 500ml carton
double cream 284ml carton, softly whipped
lemon 1, zested
stem ginger in syrup 4 pieces from a jar,
    shredded, plus 2 tbsp syrup from the jar
ginger wine 3 tbsp
ginger biscuits 10, crushed

■ Line a small loaf tin or terrine mould with cling film.

■ Mix together the yoghurt, cream, lemon zest, ginger pieces, ginger syrup and ginger wine (if using). Put ⅓ of the yoghurt mix into the bottom of the tin then add half the biscuits. Add another ⅓ of yoghurt then top with the rest of the biscuits. Finish with the rest of the yoghurt mix. Freeze for at least 4 hours or overnight.

■ Turn out and leave for 20–30 minutes before cutting into slices to serve. Serve with a little extra ginger syrup poured over and a few extra bits of ginger. **Serves 6**

The ginger wine in this terrine really intensifies the ginger flavour but you can leave it out, if you prefer.

Milk chocolate and pecan torte

30 minutes + chilling

pecans 200g, toasted and chopped
butter 300g, 125g melted, 175g softened
milk chocolate 250g
plain chocolate 250g, plus a little extra, for decorating
caster sugar 150g
eggs 6
vanilla extract 1 tbsp
double cream 568ml carton

■ Mix the pecans and melted butter together in a bowl. Pour into a 22cm springform cake tin and press down. Chill while making the rest of recipe.

■ Melt the chocolate in 20-second blasts in the microwave, or in a glass bowl set over but not in a pan of simmering water. Combine the sugar and softened butter in the bowl of an electric mixer or use a hand mixer. Beat on medium speed until fluffy, then add the eggs and mix for 2 minutes.

■ Whisk in the melted chocolate, vanilla, 125ml cream and beat for another 2 minutes. Spread this over the nut mix in the cake tin and chill for at least 3 hours. Just before serving, softly whip the remaining cream and spread it on top of the chocolate layer, then scatter with extra shaved plain chocolate. Slice and serve.

Serves 12

The butter may look like it's splitting when whipping the eggs and sugar, but it all comes together with the chocolate.

Apple and mint sorbet

35 minutes + churning

sugar 2 tbsp
mint 1 small bunch
apples 6–8, quartered and juiced to make
    850ml
lemon ½, juiced

■ Put the sugar in a small pan with 150ml water. Heat until the sugar has dissolved then add the mint. Leave to infuse for 20 minutes. Strain and add to the apple and lemon juice.

■ Pour into an ice-cream maker and churn to a sorbet consistency. **Makes 1 litre**

If you haven't got a juicer, you can buy freshly pressed apple juice in cartons.

Baked maple and walnut figs with vanilla mascarpone

30 minutes

ripe figs 12
butter 50g, cubed
walnut halves 50g
maple syrup 4 tbsp
mascarpone 200g, mixed with 1 tsp vanilla
    extract, to serve

■ Heat the oven to 200C/fan 180C/gas 6. Cut a cross into each fig about ¾ of the way down so they fan out a little. Put a cube of butter inside each fig and put in a buttered baking dish. Scatter the walnuts over and drizzle with maple syrup. Bake for about 20 minutes, glazing with the syrup and butter. Serve 3 figs per person with a dollop of the vanilla mascarpone. **Serves 4**

Ripe figs will smell fragrant and give when pressed gently.

Winter berry trifle

20 minutes + chilling

frozen mixed berries 500g bag
golden caster sugar 4 tbsp
crème de cassis 4 tbsp (or any other berry
    liqueur)
Madeira cake about 250g, sliced
mascarpone 250ml carton
fresh custard 500ml carton
vanilla extract 2 tsp
double cream 284ml + 142ml carton

■ Put the berries and sugar in a pan and heat gently until the sugar has dissolved. Stir in the cassis and cool slightly.

■ Put a layer of Madeira cake in the bottom of a large glass trifle dish and spoon over ²/₃ of the berry mix (you might not need all the liquid).

■ Beat the mascarpone until smooth then gradually beat in the custard and stir in the vanilla. Spoon on top of the cake and berries. Whip the cream to soft peaks and dollop on to the custard. Chill for an hour. Just before serving, spoon over the rest of the berry mix. **Serves 8**

You can mix and match the fillings for this trifle. Try lemon or chocolate cake instead of Madeira and use fresh strawberries as the fruit in the summer.

Redcurrant and sweet wine granita

30 minutes + freezing

redcurrants 300g
caster sugar 100g, plus extra to taste
orange 1, zested and juiced
sweet dessert wine such as muscat, 1 glass

■ Put the redcurrants, sugar and orange juice and zest into a large pan with 100ml water. Cook gently for 5–10 minutes until the redcurrants have burst.

■ Whiz in a food processor or blender then push through a sieve (taste and add a little more sugar if needed). Stir in the wine. Pour into a large baking dish and freeze for at least 4 hours.

■ Fork through the granita to break it up, then spoon into small glasses to serve.

Serves 4

The amount of sugar you need depends on the sharpness of the redcurrants you have.

Baked vanilla apricots

1 hour 20 minutes

---

unsalted butter for greasing
fresh apricots 800g, halved and stoned
golden caster sugar 2 tbsp
unwaxed lemon 1, zested into strips and
    juiced
vanilla pod 1
sweet white wine 200 ml, such as muscat
vanilla ice cream or **crème fraîche** to serve

■ Heat the oven to 180C/fan 160C/gas 4.
Butter the inside of an ovenproof dish and
add the apricots, cut-side up in a single
layer and scatter over the sugar. Add the
lemon juice and zest.

■ Split the vanilla pod in half and tuck in
among the fruit.

■ Pour over the sweet wine and cook on
the middle shelf of the oven for about
40 minutes until the fruit is tender and the
liquid reduced to a syrup. Serve warm with
vanilla ice cream or crème fraîche. **Serves 4**

Keep testing your fruit for doneness – the
riper they are the less time they will take.

Pineapple frozen yoghurt and raspberry sorbet

1 hour 40 minutes + overnight freezing

PINEAPPLE YOGHURT
pineapple 1 small ripe one, about 350g
caster sugar 125g, plus 1 tbsp
natural yoghurt 500ml
limes 2, zested and juiced
mint leaves a handful, chopped

RASPBERRY SORBET
caster sugar 200g
raspberries 500g

■ To make the pineapple yoghurt, peel and core the pineapple and whiz the flesh in a food processor to make a purée. Mix the sugar, yoghurt, lime zest, juice and mint together in a mixing bowl and add the pineapple purée. Pour into an ice-cream maker, churn until thick and then freeze.

■ To make the raspberry sorbet, boil the sugar and 150ml water for 1 minute. Set aside a few raspberries to decorate and stew the rest in the sugar syrup for 15 minutes on a medium heat. Purée in a blender or food processor. Sieve to remove the seeds and leave to cool. Chill until cold.

■ Pour into an ice-cream maker, churn until thick then freeze. To serve, soften both ices in the fridge for 20 minutes before scooping. **Serves 6**

Both of these ice creams can be made without an ice-cream maker. Simply pour them into containers, freeze partially, stir vigorously and then freeze again.

Lemon panna cotta with lemon caramel

30 minutes + cooling and setting

sunflower oil for greasing

full-fat milk 375ml

double cream 375ml

lemon 1, zested in thick strips

caster sugar 100g

gelatine 4 leaves soaked in cold water until soft

LEMON CARAMEL

caster sugar 100g

lemon juice 1 tbsp (from the zested lemon)

These taste just as good without the caramel, if you want a simpler pud.

■ Brush 6 x 150ml pudding moulds with a little sunflower oil. Put the milk and cream in a pan. Add the lemon zest and sugar, bring slowly to the boil then remove from the heat.

■ Pour 150ml of the milk mix into a small bowl, add the gelatine and stir until it has completely dissolved. Leave the rest of the mixture to cool to room temp and infuse with the zest. Stir the 2 mixtures together and strain through a fine sieve into the moulds. Chill until set.

■ Meanwhile, to make the caramel, heat the sugar in a pan until it melts and turns a golden colour – you may need to swirl the pan to keep the colour even. Take off the heat and add the lemon juice – it will splutter. Re-melt the caramel if it has hardened in lumps and then drizzle on to a piece of baking parchment on a chopping board. Cool and break into pieces. Serve the panna cotta turned out on to plates with the caramel pieces. **Makes 6**

Marbled honeycomb and chocolate mousse pots

20 minutes

milk chocolate 200g
Cadbury Crunchie 2 x 35g bars, roughly
    chopped
double cream 284ml carton
mascarpone 250ml carton

■ Melt 150g of the chocolate, then stir in the Crunchie pieces.

■ Gently stir the cream into the mascarpone then stir in the chocolate mix until just marbled. Spoon into small glasses or cups, and top with the rest of the chocolate, grated or shaved. **Serves 6**

You could serve this as a sweet canapé either in shot glasses or in dollops on china spoons.

Pink grapefruit and ginger granita

10 minutes + freezing

pink grapefruit juice 750ml
root ginger 1 thumb-sized piece, finely
    grated
caster sugar 150g
Angostura bitters 7 drops (optional)

■ Gently heat the grapefruit juice, ginger and sugar together in a pan, stirring until the sugar dissolves, but not allowing the mixture to boil. Leave to cool.

■ Strain and add the Angostura bitters (if using). Pour the mixture into a shallow container (about 20cm x 30cm) and put in the freezer for 1 hour. Use a fork to scrape the frozen edges of the granita into the slushy middle and freeze for a further hour. Repeat this process every hour for 3 or 4 hours then freeze for another hour until the granita has set. You should have a container of pink, glassy crystals. Scrape through with a fork before serving in chilled glasses. **Serves 6**

Freshly squeezed grapefruit juice has a vibrant quality, but if you need an easy dessert you will still get a great result with a carton of juice.

Mini baked Alaska

20 minutes + chilling

Madeira or **sponge cake** 1
good-quality raspberry jam 3 tbsp (without
   seeds if you prefer)
vanilla ice cream 1 carton
egg whites 6
golden caster sugar 250g

■ Cut the cake into 6 thick slices and cut
a circle out of each. Spread ½ tsp jam over
each circle and put on a baking sheet lined
with baking parchment. Put a scoop of ice
cream on to each piece of cake and freeze
for an hour or until you are ready to serve.
■ Heat the oven to 200C/fan 180C/gas 6.
Whisk the egg whites to soft peaks and
add the sugar in 4 batches, whisking as
you go until you have a stiff, shiny mixture
(this will sit in the fridge for a few hours).
■ Cover each Alaska with a thick layer of
meringue, making it nice and spiky. Bake for
3–4 minutes, the meringue should brown
slightly without the ice cream melting.
Makes 6

If you have a blowtorch you could
just brown the meringue all over
without baking.

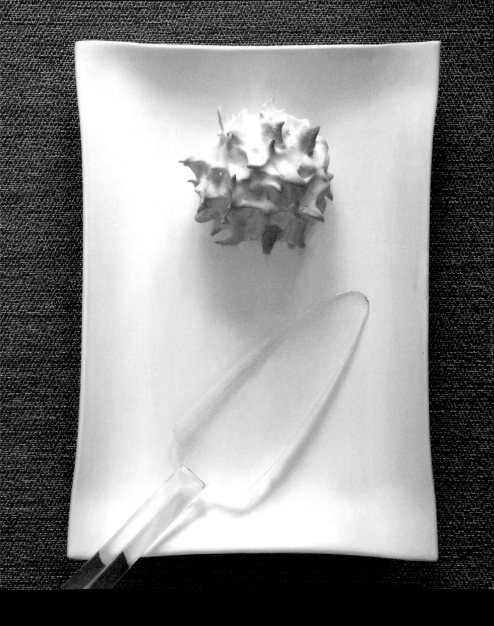

Raspberry lime curd tart

1 hour

shortcrust pastry 350g, fresh or frozen
egg yolks 3
caster sugar 125g
unsalted butter 50g, melted
half-fat crème fraîche 250ml
plain flour 2 tbsp
lime 1, zested and juiced
raspberries 150g
cream or **ice cream** to serve

■ Heat the oven to 200C/fan 180C/gas 6. Roll out the pastry on a floured surface to ½cm thick and use to line a 23cm loose-based tart tin. Line with baking parchment and baking beans or dried beans and blind bake for 10 minutes. Remove the baking parchment and bake for 5 more minutes or until the pastry looks dry and lightly golden. Turn the oven down to 180C/fan 160C/gas 4.

■ Whisk the egg yolks, sugar, melted butter, crème fraîche, flour, lime zest and juice together in a bowl, with a pinch of salt and pour into the pastry case.

■ Sprinkle over the raspberries and cook for 30–40 minutes, or until the filling is just set. Allow to cool completely on a wire rack and serve at room temperature or chilled with cream or ice cream. **Serves 8**

The filling for this tart miraculously turns into lime curd in the oven. You could replace the raspberries with blueberries or blackberries.

Champagne and elderflower jellies

15 minutes + cooling and setting

leaf gelatine 5 sheets
Champagne or **sparkling wine** 1 bottle
caster sugar 75g
elderflower cordial 2 tbsp

■ Soak the gelatine in cold water until softened. Put 100ml water and ¼ of the Champagne in a pan with the caster sugar.

■ Heat gently until the sugar has dissolved then squeeze the excess water from the gelatine sheets and stir into the liquid. Strain into a bowl, leave until cooled then add the rest of the Champagne and the cordial.

■ Divide the jelly among 6 Champagne glasses. Chill for about 4 hours (or overnight) to set. **Serves 6**

Add an elegant spoon to each of the glasses so it sets in the jelly for a stylish finish.

Limoncello syllabub with crushed amaretti

20 minutes

lemons 2, zested and juiced
limoncello liqueur 75ml
double cream 300ml
caster sugar 100g
amaretti biscuits 12, to decorate

■ Mix together the lemon juice, most of the zest and the limoncello. Pour the cream into a large bowl and softly whip with the sugar. Drizzle in the lemon mixture and whisk until incorporated.

■ Divide among 6 small glasses and chill for at least an hour. Just before serving, put 6 biscuits in a plastic bag. Crush with a rolling pin and sprinkle over each dessert with a little lemon zest. If you like, serve each with a biscuit. **Makes 6**

It's very important not to over-whip the cream, so whisk it until it's just starting to thicken then add the lemon mixture. Once you've whisked it again it will be at the perfect consistency.

Chocolate St Emilion slice

20 minutes + chilling

plain chocolate 300g
milk 150ml
golden syrup 150g
unsalted butter 140g, chopped
egg 1, lightly beaten
amaretti biscuits 150g, broken into pieces
meringue nests 3, broken into pieces
cocoa for dusting

Due to its heart-stopping list of ingredients, it's best to serve this in small portions. You have been warned.

■ Line a 23 x 13cm loaf tin with cling film so that it hangs over the edges.

■ Break the chocolate into pieces and combine with the milk, syrup, butter and a pinch of salt in a wide pan. Warm gently over a very low heat until everything has melted.

■ Stir in the egg slowly to allow it to cook slightly in the chocolate mix before removing the pan from the heat. Fold the broken biscuits and meringue into the chocolate, being careful not to crush them too much – you want whole pieces in the finished terrine to give it texture.

■ Pour the mixture into the lined loaf tin, smooth the top with a spatula and tap the tin a few times to force any air bubbles to the surface. Cover with the overhanging cling film and chill for at least 4 hours until firm.

■ Dust with cocoa and slice thinly to serve, allowing the slices to come up to room temperature for a few minutes before serving. **Serves 10**

Iced chocolate and macadamia dacquoise

1½ hours + freezing

macadamia nuts 100g, lightly toasted + chopped
caster sugar 300g
egg whites 3

GANACHE FILLING
double cream 150ml, plus extra to serve
plain or **milk chocolate** 100g, melted
half-fat crème fraîche 100g

A dacquoise is just a fancy name for a layered nutty-meringue cake. There's a bit of work involved but you can get everything done in advance – it will keep in the freezer for up to a week.

■ Heat the oven to 150C/fan 130C/gas 2. Line 2 baking sheets with baking parchment and draw 6 x 9cm-circles on each.
■ Spread 60g of macadamia on a lightly oiled sheet of foil. Heat 150g sugar with 4 tbsp water until dissolved.Boil until it turns a deep amber colour and quickly pour over the nuts. Cool and break into shards.
■ Whiz the remaining macadamia nuts in a food processor until finely ground.
■ Whisk the egg whites with a pinch of salt until stiff. Gradually add 150g sugar and whisk until firm and glossy.
■ Fold in the ground nuts. Put a spoonful of meringue on to each circle and spread carefully to fill. Bake for 45 minutes. Cool
■ Meanwhile, to make the ganache filling, softly whip the double cream then fold in the melted chocolate and crème fraîche. Spread some ganache over 4 of the meringues, top with a second meringue, repeat, finishing with meringue.
■ Freeze for at least 2 hours before serving. Allow to soften at room temperature for 10 minutes then serve with extra whipped cream and the nutty caramel shards.
Serves 4

Stem ginger fool

15 minutes

---

double cream 284ml carton
syrup from stem ginger 3 tbsp
ginger wine 4 tbsp
stem-ginger in syrup 3 pieces, 2 finely
    chopped, 1 sliced

■ Whip the cream to soft peaks, whisk in the ginger syrup and ginger wine, then stir in the chopped ginger.
■ Spoon into small glasses and top with a slice of stem ginger. **Serves 4**

You could layer this up with some crushed ginger biscuits for a different-textured pudding.

White chocolate torte with shiny chocolate sauce

30 minutes + freezing

butter 50g
amaretti biscuits 300g, finely crushed in a food processor
white chocolate 300g, chopped
whipping cream 284ml carton + 142ml carton

CHOCOLATE SAUCE
plain chocolate 100g, finely chopped
crème fraîche 125ml
caster sugar 3 tbsp

If your cream is very cold, leave it to warm up a little so it doesn't make the chocolate seize. The thicker you whisk the cream the more solid the torte will be.

■ Melt the butter in a large pan, add the biscuits and mix well. Butter an 18cm loose-based round tin and press the biscuits into the base. Freeze until cold and firm.

■ Meanwhile, melt the white chocolate in a bowl set over a pan of simmering water or in short blasts in the microwave and leave to cool.

■ Whisk the cream until you can leave a ribbon-like trail for a couple of seconds. Add 2 tbsp of the whipped cream to the white chocolate and stir it in. Pour the rest of the chocolate into the cream and mix well. Pour into the tin and chill until firm.

■ Make the sauce by putting all the ingredients in a pan with 250ml water and bring to a simmer, stirring. Simmer until the mixture thickens (enough to draw a line through it on the back of a wooden spoon) and then cool. Use some to decorate the top of the torte and re-warm the rest when ready to serve. **Serves 8**

Index

Picture and recipe credits

BBC Books and **olive** magazine would like to thank the following for providing photographs. While every effort has been made to trace and acknowledge all photographers, we would like to apologize should there be any errors or omissions.

Jean Cazals p55, p65, p71, p73, p105, p141, p171, p173, p191, p197, p201, p209, p211; Gus Filgate p11, p13, p67, p97, p137, p163, p195, p199, p205, p207; Gareth Morgans p59; David Munns p 15, p17, p21, p69, p89, p91, p103, p119, p121, p169, p189; Myles New p19, p29, p75, p99, p127, p167, p177; Michael Paul p23, p27, p63, p81, p107, p111, p117, p143, p151, p155, p203; Brett Stevens p35, p39, p43, p47,

p51, p53, p79, p93, p95, p101, p125, p139, p179, p185; Philip Webb p25, p31, p33, p37, p45, p49, p57, p61, p77, p87, p109, p113, p115, p123, p129, p131, p145, p147, p149, p153, p161, p165, p175, p181, p183, p187, p193; Simon Wheeler p41, p83, p85, p133, p135, p157, p159

All the recipes in this book have been created by the editorial team at **olive** magazine.